Conrad Weiser Homestead

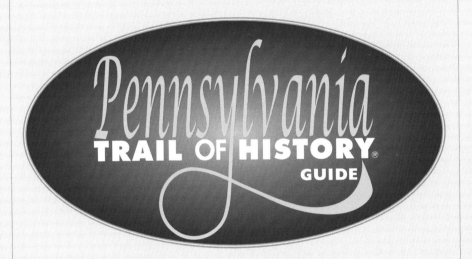

Text by John Bradley
Photographs by Kyle R. Weaver

STACKPOLE BOOKS

PENNSYLVANIA HISTORICAL
AND MUSEUM COMMISSION

Kyle R. Weaver, Series Editor
Tracy Patterson, Designer

Published by
STACKPOLE BOOKS
5067 Ritter Road
Mechanicsburg, Pennsylvania 17055

Pennsylvania Trail of History® is a registered trademark of the Pennsylvania Historical and Museum Commission.

Printed in the United States of America
2 4 6 8 10 9 7 5 3 1
FIRST EDITION

Maps by Caroline Stover

Photography
Kyle R. Weaver: cover, 3, 5, 25, 26, 28, 30, 31, 36, 39, 41–47

Library of Congress Cataloging-in-Publication Data

Bradley, John.
    Conrad Weiser Homestead / text by John Bradley ; photographs by Kyle R. Weaver—1st ed.
        p. cm.—(Pennsylvania trail of history guides)
    Includes bibliographical references.
    ISBN 0-8117-2739-4
    1. Conrad Weiser House (Womelsdorf, Pa.) 2. Womelsdorf (Pa.)—Buildings, structures, etc. 3. Weiser, Conrad, 1696–1760. 4. Pioneers—Pennsylvania—Biography. 5. Frontier and pioneer life—Pennsylvania. 6. Pennsylvania—History—Colonial period, ca. 1600–1775. 7. Indians of North America—Pennsylvania. I. Title. II. Series.

    F159.W82 B73 2001
    974.8'16—dc21

                                                                              2001020224

Contents

Editor's Preface

For more than half a century, the Pennsylvania Historical and Museum Commission (PHMC) has successfully fulfilled a mandate from the Pennsylvania state government to foster public interest in the commonwealth's history. The commission persists in that course by joining with Stackpole Books—a publisher in Pennsylvania for more than seventy years—to promote the state's historic sites and museums through a series of guidebooks, the Pennsylvania Trail of History Guides. Stackpole is proud to continue the series with this publication.

The series was conceived and created by Stackpole Books with the cooperation of the PHMC's Division of Publications and Bureau of Historic Sites and Museums. Donna Williams heads the latter, and she and her staff of professionals review the text of each guidebook for historical accuracy and have made many valuable recommendations. Diane Reed, Chief of Publications, has facilitated relations between the PHMC and Stackpole from the project's inception, organized the review process with the commission, and attended to numerous details related to the venture.

James A. Lewars, Administrator of both Conrad Weiser Homestead and Daniel Boone Homestead, has been a vital source of encouragement to me since I began developing the series in 1998. His vast knowledge of the subjects of his sites, as well as of Berks County history and early American architecture, has been integral to the precision of the Boone guidebook and this one. Michael Emery, Museum Educator at Weiser, led me to several sources for illustrations, coordinated research for the text writer, and prepared displays in the house for the photographer.

The author of the text, John Bradley, is a Pennsylvania historian and teacher who has already contributed to the series with a manuscript for *Ephrata Cloister*. In this guidebook, he provides a vivid biography of Weiser and an overview of his work as negotiator of treaties between the proprietors of Pennsylvania and the Iroquois Confederacy, emphasizing Weiser's role as peacekeeper on the frontier for two decades. He follows with a history of the homestead and a tour of the park that commemorates this pivotal figure of Colonial American history.

Kyle R. Weaver, Editor
Stackpole Books

Introduction to the Site

The Conrad Weiser Homestead preserves the property
that was home to the Colonial diplomat who medi-
ated relations with the Iroquois Indians, contributing
to the "Long Peace" that provided security for Pennsylvania's residents in the early eighteenth century. Administered
by the Pennsylvania Historical and Museum Commission,
the site was developed in the early twentieth century as a
memorial park to Weiser.

Designed by nationally prominent landscape architects, the park, with its serpentine drives, wide expanses
of lawn, majestic trees, monuments, and other fascinating
features, now bears little resemblance to the Colonial-era
frontier farm it was once part of. To the visitor, however,
the site offers a glimpse at early preservation efforts, details
on the everyday lives of rural Pennsylvania German families, and an appreciation of Conrad Weiser's vital role in
American history.

Conrad Weiser and Frontier Diplomacy

During America's Colonial period, Pennsylvania's settlers enjoyed nearly seventy-five years of peaceful relationships with their Indian neighbors. Although William Penn's benevolent policies started this era of intercultural harmony, a German immigrant named Conrad Weiser played a major role in maintaining the peace that set Pennsylvania apart from England's other colonies.

In his lifetime, Conrad Weiser crossed an ocean on an immigrant sailing ship and walked the length and breadth of Pennsylvania, his new home. Once he nearly froze to death. He mingled with Colonial governors, missionaries, and scientists, and he slept in bark-covered Iroquois longhouses. Weiser was a farmer, merchant, tanner of leather, father of fourteen children, and founder of a city and a county. He spoke three languages and wrote copiously in two of them. A spiritual man, Weiser followed several religious paths, until he returned to the Lutheran faith of his childhood. He negotiated peace, and he commanded a battalion in the French and Indian War. He could calculate the value of wampum, and he enjoyed fine organ music. He was truly one of early Pennsylvania's most remarkable citizens.

Conrad Weiser was born in 1696 in Affstat, a village near Stuttgart, in the former German kingdom of Württemberg. By the time Conrad was four years old, his parents, Johan Conrad and Anna Magdalena, had moved their family to Gross Aspach, the Weiser family's ancestral home, north of Stuttgart. Here, in the center of a farming and wine-making community, Johan Conrad worked as a baker.

Like its neighboring region, the German Palatinate, Württemberg in the early eighteenth century was still suffering from the terrible wars that swept central Europe for many years. Religious persecution was rampant, poverty was widespread, and people were restless, looking for an escape and a new start. Soon migrants were on the move, multitudes heading east to Hungary, Russia, and the Ukraine. To others, Britain's New World colonies beckoned.

In 1709, tragedy struck the Weiser household when Anna Magdalena died while pregnant with her fifteenth child.

Conrad Weiser accompanied Moravian missionary leader Count Nicholas Ludwig von Zinzendorf, left, to Shamokin in 1742 to meet with representatives of the Iroquois Confederacy. In this painting by Anna Arndt, after an original by J.V. Haidt, Shikellamy, the Iroquois spokesman, presents a string of wampum to a bearded man, who is most likely a representation of Conrad Weiser. UNITY ARCHIVES, HERRNHUT, GERMANY

The Eastern Woodland Indians. *By the early eighteenth century, the powerful Iroquois Confederacy had subjugated all of the Native American tribes of Pennsylvania. This painting depicts the ritual of storytelling that was a vital part of their culture.* I HAVE SOMETHING TO SAY (1998) BY ROBERT GRIFFING

Less than two months later, Johan Conrad and eight of his children left Württemberg for England and then crossed the Atlantic. Their destination? Queen Anne's Royal colony of New York, where workers to raise hemp and produce tar and pitch on Hudson Valley estates were in high demand.

Young Conrad's first American home was on Robert Livingston's manor near the present town of Esopus, located about one hundred miles north of New York City. Here the Weisers settled with a community of other Germans, who quickly learned that tar making would not be possible in New York; Livingston's pine trees were not the right type. The newcomers were in debt for the cost of the voyage, so they scattered, with

about 150 families heading farther north to the Schoharie Valley, forty miles west of Albany, where they settled in 1712.

Johan Conrad emerged as a leader of the fledgling frontier community in the Schoharie region. He insisted that each family obtain a secure title to its land, and he stressed the need for orderliness if the settlement hoped to survive. Before long, a forty-house hamlet called Weiserdorf ("Weiser's Village") was built near a point where several trails crossed. These paths were early highways cut through the woods by the Schoharie's original settlers, the Mohawk Indians, one of the tribes of the powerful Iroquois Confederacy, who still lived in the area.

Several Mohawk villages, known as "castles," were located near Weiserdorf, and members of the two societies soon developed good relationships. Conrad, by now an adventurous teenager, was sent to live with the family of a Mohawk named Quaynant and spent the winter of 1712–13 with them in the small village of Eskaharie. This unique experience gave him a start at learning the Mohawks' language and observing their culture, which was vastly different from anything he had seen before. He remembered being cold and hungry much of the time he spent with his hosts in their longhouse, a rectangular structure built of poles covered with tree bark, which they shared with several other families. In following years, Weiser enhanced his knowledge of Mohawk by serving as an interpreter and go-between for the German and Indian communities. He also built relationships with Mohawk leaders that would be helpful to him later.

As they had at Livingston's Manor, the Weiserdorf settlers struggled to survive in the Schoharie Valley. After about ten years, in 1723, fifteen families departed, heading south past New York's provincial border toward a brighter destination: Pennsylvania. The Quaker colony's humane founder, William Penn, had died several years earlier, and his sons were now the proprietors of this huge block of prime real estate. Like their visionary father, the Penn brothers were actively recruiting settlers. Believing Germans to be honest, hardworking, and dependable, the Penns guided the Schoharie emigrants toward Tulpehocken, a frontier valley northwest of Philadelphia.

There were no Weisers among those making the 1723 exodus to Pennsylvania. In that year, Conrad marked the third anniversary of his wedding to Anna Eva Feg, a German-born Schoharie settler like himself. Their first son, Philip, was already one year old. Soon

CHRONOLOGY

1696	Conrad Weiser is born in Württemberg, Germany, on November 2
1709–10	Family emigrates to America, settles in New York
1712	Weisers move to Schoharie Valley, near Albany, New York
1713	Conrad spends winter with a Mohawk family
1720	Marries Anna Eva Feg
1729	Moves to Pennsylvania, settles in the Tulpehocken region on farm now known as Conrad Weiser Homestead
1731	Goes to Philadelphia with Shikellamy to interpret at treaty
1732	With James Logan and Shikellamy, creates Pennsylvania's new Indian policy
1735	Becomes involved with Seventh-Day Baptist community at Ephrata
1737	Barely survives difficult winter journey to Onondaga, center of the Six Nations of the Iroquois
1741	Becomes a justice of the peace for northern Lancaster County
1744	Interprets at Lancaster Treaty
1748	Attends Logstown Treaty in western Pennsylvania; helps develop town of Reading
1750	Builds house in Reading on Penn Square
1754	Attends Albany Congress with Benjamin Franklin
1756	Becomes lieutenant colonel, 1st Battalion, Pennsylvania Regiment
1756–58	Attends series of conferences at Easton
1760	Dies at home in Tulpehocken Valley, on July 13, at age sixty-three

Philip had a baby sister, Anna Magdalena. In 1727, Anna Maria was born, and the next year, little Frederick joined the family. In February 1729, this family of six pulled up stakes in New York and set off for Tulpehocken.

Located in today's Lebanon and Berks Counties, the Tulpehocken Valley offered the Weisers more fertile soil, a milder climate, and a longer growing season than Schoharie's farmlands. Starting with a two-hundred-acre tract that lay at the base of Eagle's Peak, a prominent outcropping of the South Mountains, Conrad carved some fields out of the forest and began the cycle of planting and harvest that shaped the life of the valley. This was a predominantly German section of a province that was less than fifty years old, but was already known as "the best poor man's country," the place most likely, in either the Old World or the New, to give the average person a comfortable, secure life.

James Logan was provincial secretary of Pennsylvania and the representative of the proprietors in affairs with the Native Americans. CONRAD WEISER HOMESTEAD

WEISER AND THE INDIANS

Weiser's career as an interpreter and negotiator with the Indians began in late 1731, when he was visited by a group of Iroquois who were traveling to Philadelphia. Heading for a meeting with provincial leaders in colonial Pennsylvania's capital, the Iroquois wanted someone who was comfortable with both their language and English. The Indians' spokesman, Shikellamy (pronounced "Shih-KELL-a-mee"), asked Weiser to translate for them at the upcoming conference. Probably wondering if his skills in his second and third languages were adequate, the German-American from Tulpehocken agreed to go along. This decision not only changed Weiser's life, but also altered the relationship between Europeans and Indians in Pennsylvania forever.

The conference brought together three persons who would have a significant impact on Pennsylvania's Indian policy over the following decades. Shikellamy represented the Iroquois, a powerful Indian confederation centered in New York that controlled many other native people, including the tribes of Pennsylvania. The colony's spokesman was Irish-born James Logan, provincial secretary and advisor to the Penn family. Conrad Weiser was the third. Together this trio dismantled Pennsylvania's old Indian policy and replaced it with a new one.

The old policy was started in 1681 by William Penn, founder of the province. Penn knew that earlier English settlements had experienced violent conflicts with the Indians they encountered. In 1622, an uprising by the Powhatans almost destroyed Jamestown. New England saw the bloody Pequot War in the 1630s. And only five years before Penn received his provincial charter, Bacon's Rebellion convulsed Virginia, resulting in great losses for the Susquehannocks and for the colony's coastal tribes. In

WEISER'S PARTNERS IN INDIAN DIPLOMACY

Pennsylvania's new Indian policy of the 1730s grew out of the collaboration of Conrad Weiser; James Logan, who represented the province's government; and Shikellamy, spokesman for the Six Nations of the Iroquois.

James Logan was born in County Armagh, Ireland, in 1674, but he was of Scottish ancestry. His father, a schoolmaster, was a minister in the Church of England until he converted to Quakerism. James learned Latin, Greek, and Hebrew before he was thirteen; taught in a school in Bristol, England; and became involved in the shipping business in his late teens. Then he met William Penn, the proprietor of Pennsylvania, who hired Logan to be his secretary.

In 1699, Logan accompanied Penn on one of his rare visits to the colony. Before long, Logan was appointed provincial secretary and clerk of the provincial council. These were the first of many posts he held in Pennsylvania's government in a career than spanned fifty-two years, including commissioner of property, receiver general, council member, mayor of Philadelphia, judge, and chief justice of the colony's supreme court.

Because of his success in trading with the Indians and his profitable investments in land, Logan became a wealthy man. He and his wife, Sarah Read, and their five children lived in luxury at Stenton, their estate in Germantown. Here Logan kept his magnificent library of three thousand books. At Stenton, he also pursued scientific studies, writing treatises on botany, astronomy, and meteorology. Logan died in 1751.

Shikellamy's biography is more sketchy. His birthdate is unknown, and his parentage is cloudy. He was adopted by the Oneida nation of the Iroquois, but his group of origin is a mystery. Even his precise name is a puzzle, for at different times he was known as *Ungquater-ughiathe*, *Takashwangaroras*, and *Swateney*, which may be a variation of *Onkhiswathetani*. Shikellamy is probably the Delaware or English version of an Oneida name.

Shikellamy first appeared in Pennsylvania in 1728, one year before Conrad Weiser moved to Tulpehocken. He had a wife, five sons, and two daughters. By 1737, his family was living at Shamokin, the Indian village on the Susquehanna River at the site of today's city of Sunbury.

In 1744, Shikellamy owned a new house at Shamokin that measured fifty by eighteen feet. He was being courted by Moravian missionaries, who built him a blacksmith's shop and persuaded him to teach them the Oneida language. Following the tragic deaths by illness of eleven of his family members, Shikellamy converted to the Moravian faith in 1748. At his death in December of that year, he was survived by a son, Soyechtowa, whose English name was James Logan.

that same year of 1676, King Philip's War ended in the near obliteration of the Wampanoags and Narragansetts of New England.

Penn, the proprietor, signaled his sincere desire to have peaceful relationships with Pennsylvania's Indians in a letter of friendship he wrote in October 1681. "It is my resolution to live justly, peaceably, and friendly with you," Penn told the "Kings of the Indians of Pennsylvania." A positive way to ensure peace among the new settlers and first residents of the colony, Penn reasoned, was for the Europeans to agree to buy the land from the Indians. Although his monarch, Charles II, had granted him every square inch of Pennsylvania, Penn acknowledged that the Indians were the "true lords of the soil." It followed, then, that only after the Indians had given their permission could ownership of the land be transferred to English colonists.

Several Indian groups lived in Pennsylvania at the time of first contact with Europeans. In the east, in the valleys of the Delaware and Lehigh Rivers, lived the Lenape, also known as Delawares. The Shawnee were found in northeastern and central Pennsylvania, and the Susquehannocks lived in the valley of the great river system that bears their name. In the west were Eries and Wyandots, while other groups such as Nanticokes and Conoys were moving into the colony from other regions.

The thirteen British colonies of North America developed their own individual Indian policies by default, for no instructions came from London on the subject of relationships with the native inhabitants. Most colonists saw the Indians as violent heathen savages, despising them as threats to the security of the new settlements. Though willing to trade for furs and other riches the Indians might possess, Europeans were not prepared to admit them to membership in their communities. Few could have written a letter like Penn's, which concluded with the phrase "I am your friend" inscribed above his signature.

The "Long Peace" that began with Penn's first land purchases endured for almost three-quarters of a century. Before the 1750s, Pennsylvania witnessed fewer Indian-European conflicts than any other colony. With its mixed population of migrants from many European nations, it was also the most diverse Colonial settlement. Penn's dream of a "Good Correspondance" among people was becoming reality.

After his death in 1718, the ownership of Penn's colony passed to his three sons by his second marriage. Honoring the goal of extending the intercultural harmony established by their father's system, the younger Penns also recognized that the policy might need some adjustment. They were guided in the formulation of this new strategy by Logan, Weiser, and Shikellamy, who constructed a basic change in Indian-European relationships.

From this point on, Pennsylvania officials would stop purchasing land and making other agreements with the various Indian groups who lived in the colony. Instead, they would talk directly with the native people who had conquered Pennsylvania's Indians and who ruled over them: the Iroquois. One benefit of this policy change was practical: Dealing exclusively with the Iroquois would simplify the province's bargaining with Indians. Second, and more importantly, the new policy would pull Pennsylvania and the Iroquois into a closer relationship.

THE IROQUOIS

From their homeland in upper New York, the Iroquois, or *Kanonsionni*, as they called themselves, ruled an empire of many subject peoples in what is now the northeastern United States. Despite a rather small population of about fifteen thousand, they were reckoned to be the most powerful Indian group in the entire North Atlantic region. The Iroquois' strength came partly from their crucial position halfway between English colonies to the east and French settlers to the west. Another factor was the aggressive military tradition that pervaded their culture. Finally, their innovative political structure supplied order, structured decision making, and assured internal harmony.

Although the date cannot be determined with precision, years before Europeans landed on North America's coasts to claim the land for themselves, five related *Kanonsionni* nations formed an alliance. Neighbors, they drew on the bonds of similar languages and cultures to create a confederation, much as thirteen English-speaking colonies would unite in the 1770s to fight for freedom.

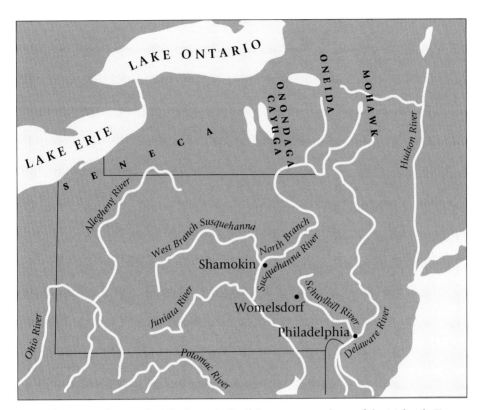

Pennsylvania and Iroquoia. *The Iroquois Confederacy was made up of the Mohawk, Tuscarora, Oneida, Onondaga, Cayuga, and Seneca nations, and their lands spread through northwestern Pennsylvania and across New York. Weiser made several trips to Shikellamy's home in Shamokin and to the Iroquois central meeting place in Onondaga.*

Iroquois territory, dubbed Iroquoia by some writers, was a broad band that lay below the Great Lakes and stretched from Niagara to the Hudson River. From west to east, the people were the Seneca, the Cayuga, the Onondaga, the Oneida, and the Mohawk. Their alliance is known as the Iroquois Confederation, League of the Iroquois, or the Five Nations. (In the 1720s, the Tuscaroras, who were linguistically related, moved north from the Carolinas and joined the League, which afterward was called the Six Nations.)

As a true confederation, the League gave some power to a central governing council while permitting the individual nations the right to act independently on certain issues. Meeting at least once a year, the Great Council consisted of forty-nine chiefs, hereditary representatives of ancient clans that made up each separate nation. When it gathered at the village of Onondaga (now Syracuse, New York), at the center of Iroquoia, the council discussed matters of mutual concern, always seeking harmony among the Six Nations. The chiefs spoke freely and openly, and often at great length, before reaching decisions that were achieved by consensus.

For the Iroquois, the League was much more than a political structure, for it was based on concepts that were fundamental to their culture. Ironically, for a people who excelled at warfare, the

Iroquois prized the absence of conflict, the "Great Peace," among themselves. Their religious values encouraged cooperation, and they saw negotiation and diplomacy as the surest way to maintain sound relationships.

Within the League, power radiated downward from the Onondaga Council to lesser councils within each nation, clan, and family. Warriors voiced their opinions in councils, and women, too, had their own councils that played active roles in Iroquois society. It was women, for example, who chose the chiefs who were entitled to sit on the Great Council. By contrast, the League's power over its subject peoples, such as the Indians of Pennsylvania, was expressed in a different way. Choosing one person to oversee the conquered nations, the council would send him to live among them, both to monitor their activities and to inform them of Onondaga's wishes. For the Lenape, Shawnee, and other groups of central and eastern Pennsylvania, that resident monitor was Shikellamy.

INDIAN AGENT

In September 1736, Weiser accompanied a delegation of one hundred Indians to Philadelphia for a follow-up to the conference of 1731–32. At this gathering, friendships were renewed all around, especially among Weiser, Secretary Logan, and Shikellamy, designers of the "New Indian Policy." Pennsylvania accepted the right of the Iroquois to speak on behalf of the colony's Indians, and the League dropped its claim to the ownership of land in the lower Susquehanna Valley in return for a few guns, hats, tobacco pipes, and other items.

This agreement gave the colony clear possession of a rich new frontier region where a flood of settlers was about to enter. To Weiser went the prestige of helping achieve a compact pleasing to both sides. And the Iroquois were happy that their authority was officially recognized. They were also very pleased with their new interpreter, telling Logan that Weiser was "faithfull & honest . . . a true good Man [who] had spoke [Pennsylvania's] Words & our Words and not his own." To show its gratitude, the League gave Weiser a fine piece of leather and two deerskins.

Weiser's next adventure as an intercultural go-between became the most challenging physical ordeal of his life. It began early in 1737, when he was asked to travel to Onondaga, the meeting place of the Great Council. His mission was to persuade the Six Nations to break off a war with the Catawbas of the South. Because this conflict might catch Virginians in the crossfire, Williamsburg asked Philadelphia to use its newfound influence with the Iroquois to end the fighting. Late February was too early in the season to begin the three-hundred-mile trip, Weiser knew, but the situation was urgent.

With two companions, Weiser set off on the Tulpehocken Path, the trail that connected his farm with Shikellamy's residence in Shamokin (now Sunbury), Pennsylvania. His journey took him scrambling over or around six mountain ridges covered with ice and snow.

After a two-week delay, the party, which now included Shikellamy, resumed its northward trek through snow that was, at minimum, knee-deep. The going, which before had been merely difficult, now was arduous. By April 8, Weiser thought he had reached his limit, as he recorded in his travel journal: "This was the hardest and most fatiguing day's journey I had ever made. . . . I trembled and shook so much all over, I thought I must fall from weariness and perish. I stepped aside and sat down under a tree to die, which I hoped

THE STORY OF WEISER'S DREAM DIPLOMACY

According to an old story, one day Conrad Weiser was traveling the Susquehanna Indian Path through central Pennsylvania with Shikellamy. As they neared the Isle of Que, near Selinsgrove, Shikellamy confided: "I have had a dream. I dreamed that you gave me a new rifle." Knowing that Iroquois custom required that such a wish expressed in a dream be fulfilled, Weiser promptly handed over his firearm.

Then Weiser spoke: "I, too, have had a dream. I dreamt that you gave me that island in the river." And Shikellamy, bound to reciprocate, promptly deeded the island to his companion. But, he added, "I will never dream with you again."

This tale probably owes its origin to a documented Iroquois practice known as dream guessing. Part of the Mid-winter Festival, dream guessing involved allowing an individual to describe, in a disguised manner, an instruction or wish he or she had recently dreamed about. After listening to the disguised dream, the villagers were required to guess its true meaning, and then to grant the wish. On one occasion, a woman placed a mattock, or digging hoe, on the ground. The onlookers knew that she was asking for a small plot of ground on which to grow corn.

Similar dream stories involving Indians and Europeans were common in the eighteenth century, and they were told in various areas about different people. Weiser's journal, however, gives evidence of his participation in "dream diplomacy." In it he noted that he should buy "a wooden pipe with a civerin [covering] over it . . . to answer Saghsidowas dream."

The Iroquois believed that dreams were messages from supernatural beings. They also anticipated modern psychology's view that dreams can express subconscious desires and may hint at issues that are troubling the dreamer. Thus dream guessing played an important role in helping to cure emotional illnesses, by fulfilling, either actually or symbolically, certain hidden desires.

would be hastened by the cold approaching night." But Shikellamy persuaded Weiser to get back on his feet and resume the journey.

In a few days, the party stumbled into Onondaga, where Weiser delivered his message, setting in motion the talks that would eventually bring an end to the Iroquois-Catawba conflict. The brutal hike had paid off, and peace was ensured.

Weiser repeated his walking trip to Onondaga several more times over the next quarter century, and he traveled by foot to many other locations as well. He learned that winter was a prohibitive time to travel, the ground was too wet in spring, and summer was too hot. That left fall as the best season for a journey by Indian path. More than one hundred trails crisscrossed Pennsylvania, and some tied into an interlocking system of routes that ran to the Chesapeake Bay, Kentucky's Cumberland Gap, Detroit, or the Natchez Trace in Mississippi. Some were a mere one foot in width, although eighteen inches was more typical. Because finding food en route could be a problem, Weiser liked to go well supplied, packing beef, bacon, rice, and cheese, as well as rum, wine, chocolate, and tea. He preferred to sleep in a hammock but could rest on pine boughs as the Indians did.

In 1743, Weiser was awarded the title of Pennsylvania's "province interpreter," the only official designation relating to his career as negotiator and translator that he would receive. In that same year, he traveled once again to Onondaga, this time accompanied by cartographer Lewis Evans and noted Philadelphia botanist John Bartram. Bartram's journal of this venture, published in 1751, is a classic tale of wilderness travel.

Oswego and an Iroquois Longhouse.
Weiser traveled with John Bartram to Onondaga in 1743, and Bartram recounted the adventure in his Observations . . . In his Travels to Onondaga, Oswego and the Lake Ontario . . . , *published in London in 1751. The book included this illustration as a foldout frontispiece. The top portion is a layout of a castle, or longhouse, and shows the travelers' sleeping quarters.*
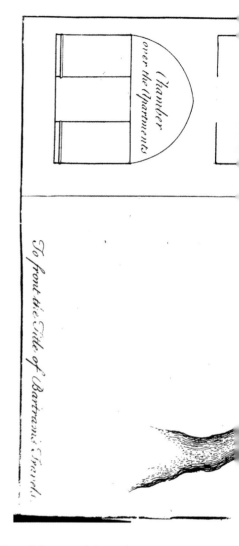

LIBRARY COMPANY OF PHILADELPHIA

Weiser took a shorter journey in the summer of 1744, when he marched twenty-five miles south to Lancaster to play a major part in a treaty, or series of negotiating sessions, with representatives of the Six Nations. Then the biggest and most important town in Pennsylvania after Philadelphia, Lancaster had been picked as the site of the 1744 treaty because it was closer to the frontier and because its courthouse was large enough to hold the several hundred expected participants and guests. The Iroquois sent a delegation of 252, led by Canasatego, an Onondaga who sat on the League council, as well as twenty-four other chiefs. Joining leaders from Penn's colony were commissioners from Maryland and Virginia.

After the representatives exchanged gifts, including strings and belts of wampum, and enjoyed a banquet, complete with alcoholic drinks and after-dinner tobacco, the serious work began. As usual, the colonies wanted more Indian land, and the Indians wanted guarantees of their right of passage through the Europeans' territories. Maryland and Virginia followed Pennsylvania's lead by acknowledging the Iroquois' authority over other Indian groups, and they paid Canasatego and his chiefs nominal sums for land cessions in the Shenandoah Valley. What

Weiser did not explain to the League representatives, however, was the clause in the treaty that transferred hundreds of thousands of acres in the Ohio Valley to Virginia, whose Colonial charter, broadly interpreted, entitled the Old Dominion to that region.

It was about the time of the Lancaster Treaty that the Iroquois began to call Weiser by a new name, *Tarachiawagon*. (Weiser's first Indian name, *Siguras*, meant "Killer.") This was a great honor, for *Tarachiawagon* was the name of an Iroquois god. The word is trans-

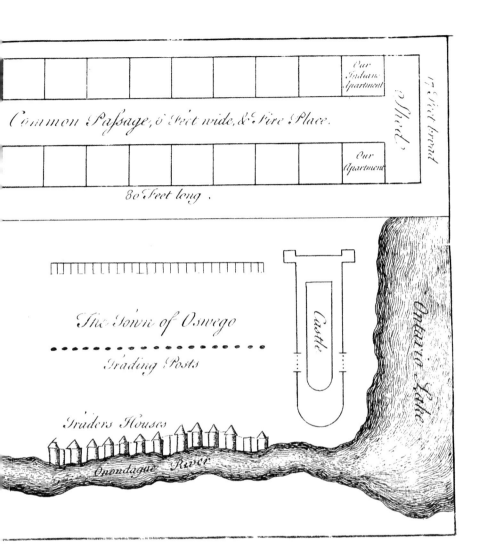

Common Passage, 6 Feet wide, & Fire Place.

Our Indian Apartment

Our Apartment

80 Feet long.

Fort brand

Short

The Town of Oswego

Trading Posts

Castle

Ontario Lake

Traders Houses

Onondague River

lated as "Holder of the Heavens" and signifies a figure of central importance in society, a powerful being who served as teacher, guide, and protector.

THE NEGOTIATOR'S ROLE
Immense cultural and language barriers separated American colonists and Indians. To cross these boundaries, skillful negotiators were needed who not only spoke both languages, but also understood the values of each society. A good mediator paid attention to differences in style, knowing, for example, that Europeans favored a businesslike brisk pace, whereas Indians preferred to move more slowly.

Conrad Weiser may have benefited from being an outsider to both the Iroquois and British societies. Encountering both cultures in his impressionable teenage years, he worked to become comfortable with each. This unique situation certainly gave German-born Weiser advantages as a negotiator. It also allowed him to empathize with both civilizations and understand cultural nuances that

THE AT THE WOODS' EDGE CEREMONY

Conrad Weiser advised his fellow Pennsylvanians that they would have to "converse with Indians & study their Genius" if the colony hoped to establish good relationships with them. One way for Europeans to draw closer to the Indians was to observe and participate in their rituals and ceremonies. In this way, the colonists could affirm the value placed on these acts by the Indians and pull the two cultures closer together.

A ritual that probably began about the time of the formation of the League of the Iroquois and then spread to other native groups in Pennsylvania was the At the Woods' Edge Ceremony. This solemn event was held in a clearing at the end of a pathway through the woods where a traveler had just emerged from an overland journey. The ceremony was designed to acknowledge the dangers and difficulties the walker had just experienced, and it would restore him, symbolically, to well-being, physically and emotionally.

Holding one or more strings of wampum, a spokesman would begin the At the Woods' Edge Ceremony by speaking of the guest's arduous journey "thro' dangerous places where evil Spirits reign." These spirits, the Indians believed, could cause slips and falls, broken bones, cuts, scratches, bumps, and bruises, and a host of other misfortunes that Europeans might have chalked up to mere accidents. Weiser's writings reveal just how dangerous woods travel could be. After one trip to Onondaga, he complained that the trip had been "enough to kill a Man to come such a Long and bad Road over Hills, Rocks, Old Trees, and Rivers."

Next, the host performed the ceremonial act of symbolically wiping the sweat from the traveler's body and pulling the painful thorns from the soles of his feet. He then proceeded to metaphorically clear the traveler's ears "from any evil Matters" and to remove dust and tears from his eyes. Finally, the traveler's mouth, throat, heart, and mind were ritually freed of "all Grief and Uneasiness," as all of the afflictions that had befallen him on his walk were washed away. The ceremony might conclude with the ritual exchange of gifts, such as belts or strings of wampum, tobacco, or European trade goods.

might have been missed by another go-between.

Weiser could converse in English and in the Mohawk variant of the Iroquoian language family. His ability with these languages was a remarkable achievement for a person who encountered both of them in the same period of his life. Specialists who teach English as a second language to teenagers today report that it usually takes five to seven years for them to speak and read it comfortably. To acquire two new languages simultaneously must have taken extreme concentration and dedication.

While many people claim that English is a difficult language to learn, it does have similarities with German because of their common ancestry. The Iroquoian family of languages, on the other hand, was totally unlike anything spoken in Europe. One of more than 350 language groupings originally spoken by indigenous people in North America, Iroquoian did not have a written form. Varieties of the language were spoken by people of the Six Nations and by other groups, such as the Hurons and Susquehannocks in the north and the Cherokee in the South. Iroquoian could have five to seven vowels and nine to eleven consonants, depending on the particular variety used by one of the subgroups.

In Mohawk, words, especially verbs, were made up of compounds and could be incredibly long. For example, the verb *ionsahatihwistanniion:ten* ("they hung the bell back up there") expresses a complete thought all in one word. To say "I'm trembling," a Mohawk speaker would say *wakya'tishonhkhwa'*. Complicating matters, sometimes speakers dropped certain syllables of lengthy words, and the emphasis or accent given to a particular word part could vary the meaning.

Mohawk sentence structure is also very different from that of English. Words appear in an order that shows their importance to the message, not one based on their roles as subjects or predicates. Finally, a new Iroquoian speaker would have to distinguish among six combining ways of saying something as simple as "we": *teni-, tewa-, iaken-, iakwa-, ionkeni-,* and *ionkwa-*. It is no wonder that William Andrews, an English missionary who met the Mohawks at the time Weiser did, reported that their language was "Extream hard to be learnt."

When the two cultures met in treaty, they followed a formula that had been developing over the years. Provincial leaders sat at one table, accompanied by scribes who attempted to record the proceedings. Facing the colonists were the Indian spokesmen, who represented only a fraction of the hundreds of Iroquois who came to the gathering. Ceremonial remarks opened the conference, with Six Nations orators giving long, eloquent speeches packed with figurative, metaphorical language. As they talked, their nimble fingers searched the strings of wampum (beads made from shells) they used as memory aids.

The crowd at a treaty gathering included Colonial aristocrats in velvet and lace, tattooed Mohawks, Quakers in plain clothes, and Lenape in face paint. Through the din of trading, feasting, and drumming, one could hear snatches of Oneida, German, Shawnee, and Gaelic. It was a "human carnival," one recent scholar has concluded. Whiskey, throbbing drums, rhythmic dancing, curious townspeople, and festive Indians all contributed to the big show.

Benjamin Franklin's impressions of a 1753 treaty in the frontier town of Carlisle, Pennsylvania, were included in his famous *Autobiography*. One of the commissioners representing the Pennsylvania legislature at this treaty, Franklin noted how much the Indians enjoyed the rum they were given at the conclusion of the meetings. On the treaty's last evening, wrote Franklin, he wandered out to the Indian encampment on the edge of town, where he saw a wild scene in the light of a giant bonfire. "Their dark-colour'd bodies, half naked, seen only by the gloomy light of the bonfire, running after and beating one another with firebrands, accompanied by their horrid yellings, form'd a scene the most resembling our ideas of hell that could well be imagin'd," reported the Philadelphian.

Weiser, as interpreter, negotiator, and agent, organized many of these treaty sessions. He was the one who had to persuade the Iroquois to at least attempt to be punctual. He had to massage the egos of Colonial leaders, reminding them to slow down the pace and not

Weiser's Seal.

talk down to the Indians. He had to find food and shelter for the ever-increasing number of Iroquois who joined the Six Nations delegations. And he had to obtain presents for the Indians, as gift giving was an important part of the ritual. At one treaty, he handed out two hundred shirts, three blankets, forty-seven guns, forty-eight mouth harps, and 18 shillings worth of vermilion dye. Though to some it may have been a "carnival," a treaty conference could be a headache for the host. It was "four weecks Spent disagreeable," Weiser complained after a 1757 meeting.

THE END OF THE LONG PEACE

As the middle of the eighteenth century approached, the European colonies in North America experienced dramatic population growth. There were one hundred thousand Pennsylvanians in 1740, and twice that number only twenty years later. This increase was a major factor pushing settlers west, across ridges and mountain chains, toward the Ohio Valley. Land speculators, traders, and fur trappers joined farmers in eyeing this western land with keen interest.

Complicating the situation was the fact that this immense territory west of the Alleghenies was claimed by several rivals. First were the Indians: Lenape and Shawnee from the east, Wyandots, and some groups related to the Iroquois. Authorities in Quebec insisted that the region was part of New France. The Penn family was certain that this land was included in Charles II's 1681 grant. But Virginia, the oldest British colony, claimed that a precise reading of its 1606 charter gave it the Ohio Country.

Weiser's first trip to the west country came in 1748, when he took part in a treaty at Logstown, an important trading center on the Ohio River near today's

borough of Ambridge. Taking gifts valued at 28 pounds sterling, Weiser attempted to obtain the right for Pennsylvanians to do business in the Ohio–Mississippi Valley system. This would open a lucrative market to the province, and Weiser made a start toward asserting Pennsylvania's presence in the region.

That same year, Weiser also lost a traveling companion, negotiating partner, and friend when Shikellamy died at Shamokin in December. This representative of the Six Nations had initiated Weiser into the give-and-take world of intercultural diplomacy, exposed him to the hazards of narrow Indian pathways, and reacquainted him with life in an Iroquois longhouse. Weiser's friendship with Shikellamy had always provided him with more credibility and a connection with the highest strata of Iroquois society. After Shikellamy's death, Weiser's influence began to wane.

The disputed Ohio Valley would lead directly to another in the long series of wars—a total of six—that took place between 1689 and 1815. Rivals for land, power, wealth, and prestige, Britain and France found no way to settle disputes except on the battlefield. In their struggles for the North American continent, the combatants frequently drew Indian groups into the conflict, with some nations favoring the French and others helping the British. The Iroquois usually chose neutrality, and although they had extended their "covenant chain" of peace to New York and Pennsylvania, the Six Nations did not fight on behalf of the English colonists.

France's grand strategy was to gain control of the water route from the mouth of the St. Lawrence, through the Great Lakes, along the Ohio, and down the Mississippi to New Orleans. At key points, such as Presqu'isle (now Erie) and at the Forks of the Ohio (Pittsburgh), the French built forts to block British access to the region. In response, New York invited representatives from other colonies to a meeting where collective efforts against the French threat could be discussed. The Albany Congress met in June and July 1754. In the eighteenth century, a "congress" was just a gathering; it had no lawmaking power. Weiser attended the congress; a fellow Pennsylvania delegate was Benjamin Franklin, who proposed a limited plan of Colonial union, including an interprovincial Parliament to discuss issues of mutual concern. Franklin's plan, which included a confederation structure loosely based on that of the Six Nations of the Iroquois, was rejected by the gathering.

The Albany Congress did succeed in renewing friendly relationships among the English colonies and the Iroquois, who had also sent delegates to the meeting. Delegates also discussed possible responses to French maneuvers in the Ohio country. In a sidebar session that was not part of the official agenda, Weiser closed a deal for his colony to buy a huge tract of land in western Pennsylvania from the Iroquois. This purchase angered the Indians who lived there, for they denied the Six Nations' right to sell the region. The congress also led Weiser to confess to having some misgivings about his role as a negotiator, for he admitted shortly afterward, "I am perplects with Indian affairs."

Meanwhile, back in the Ohio Valley, rumors of war were becoming reality, as English and French forces were attacking one another's forts, overpowering them, and forcing their garrisons to leave. For example, on July 4, 1754, a young militia commander from Virginia was driven out of Fort Necessity, located in the Great Meadows in today's Fayette County, Pennsylvania. The lieutenant

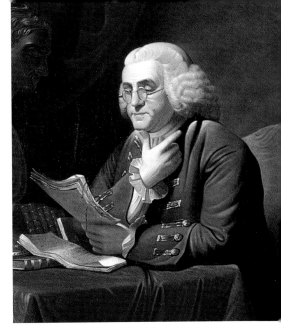

Benjamin Franklin and Weiser served together as delegates from Pennsylvania to the Albany Congress, a gathering of representatives from the colonies to discuss French fortification of disputed lands in 1754.

INDEPENDENCE NATIONAL HISTORICAL PARK

colonel who suffered the indignity of this surrender was George Washington.

In June 1755, General Edward Braddock set out with a force of twenty-two hundred British and American troops, heading for Fort Duquesne, built by the French at the spot where the Allegheny and Monongahela Rivers meet to form the Ohio. With Colonel Washington as his aide, Braddock directed his army's slow progress through the dense forests of western Pennsylvania.

Suddenly, on July 9, Braddock's force collided with a French unit from Fort Duquesne led by Capt. Daniel-Hyacinthe-Marie Lienard de Beaujeu. The French were resilient, and the British panicked. In two hours, Braddock's force suffered more than one thousand casualties. The general had four horses shot out from under him before he was carried off the field with a fatal injury. Washington did not receive so much as a scratch. The

The French and Indian War. The British objective to drive the French from western Pennsylvania was foiled when French forces and their Indian allies attacked and defeated Gen. Edward Braddock's men after they had crossed the Monongahela, near Fort Duquesne, in 1755. THE CROSSING (1995) BY ROBERT GRIFFING

conflict known to Americans as the French and Indian War was on.

After Braddock's defeat, Pennsylvania's frontiers erupted with violence, as small raiding parties of Shawnee and Lenape, often including one French officer, began to attack isolated cabins, hoping to drive the settlers off the land. Although fighting spread to other colonies, geography dictated that Pennsylvania would hold a central position in this conflict, known in Europe as the Seven Years' War. Unlike other colonies, Pennsylvania had no citizen militia. Because the Quaker-dominated Colonial legislature opposed spending money for military defense, the province was extremely vulnerable to the fast-paced, stealthy attacks of France's Indian allies. With refugees fleeing before them, the Indians pushed eastward, across the Susquehanna. Before long, their raids swept across the Blue Mountains. "We are in a dismal situation," Weiser wrote at this time to Pennsylvania's Governor Morris.

As more and more citizens joined the clamor for a defense force, the Colonial legislature finally authorized the creation of a provincial army. Weiser, who had no military training or experience, was appointed lieutenant colonel

THE OUTCOME OF
THE FRENCH AND INDIAN WAR

The French and Indian War, which ended Pennsylvania's "Long Peace" with its Indian neighbors, was the North American component of the Seven Years' War. Truly an early "world war," the Seven Years' War was fought in Europe, Africa, India, the Caribbean, and on the oceans. Complications of European power politics led Russia and Austria to ally with France, while Britain was supported by the north German state of Prussia. Although fighting in America had begun two years earlier, the war was officially declared in 1756.

Conrad Weiser played a part in this struggle as a provincial officer responsible for the defense of eastern Pennsylvania and as a diplomat who helped negotiate several treaties at Easton, the last of which was in October 1758. A month later, a combined British and Colonial force of nearly nine thousand men under the command of Gen. John Forbes advanced on the French Fort Duquesne, which had been built at the junction of the Ohio, Allegheny, and Monongahela Rivers. Before the British force could fire a shot, however, the French defenders, deprived of their Indian allies, blew up the fort with gunpowder and abandoned it. Forbes renamed the spot Fort

Pitt in honor of William Pitt, earl of Chatham, who had been placed in overall charge of the war effort by King George II. Today it lies in the heart of the city of Pittsburgh.

In 1759, three other French forts, Machault, LeBoeuf, and Presqu'isle, in western Pennsylvania, also fell to the British, as did Fort Ticonderoga in New York. On September 13 of that year, the British defeated the French on the Plains of Abraham in front of the city of Quebec. Fighting in North America virtually came to an end in 1760 when the French surrendered at Montreal on September 8 and at Detroit on November 29, only a few months after Weiser's death.

In the Treaty of Paris, signed on February 10, 1763, France gave Canada and all of the territory it had claimed south of the Great Lakes to Britain. With one stroke of a pen, the British more than doubled the size of their empire in North America. Their navy and commercial fleet were now unrivaled on the seas. But the long war had been costly, so London soon embarked on a policy of taxing its colonists to help pay off the debt. Over the next dozen years, Americans would demonstrate exactly how they felt about these new taxes.

of the 1st Battalion, Pennsylvania Regiment. His largely German five-hundred man unit, dressed in green coats with red lapels, or facings, drilled to the instructions of a British manual of arms. The battalion was deployed in a defensive posture along an arc running from the Susquehanna to the Delaware.

Weiser was also responsible for overseeing the building of several forts in the mountain ridges to the north. Among these was Fort Henry, a log stockade located near today's Berks County community of Bethel, which was completed in February 1756. In theory, these forts could shelter refugees and hold gar-

risons of troops. In harvest season, the soldiers protected farmers as they brought in their crops. From the forts, detachments of infantrymen swept out to reconnoiter ridges and valleys, searching for intruders bent on terrorizing local citizens.

Weiser's military service was brief, for he resigned his commission in 1758 and was soon back at the negotiating table. In a series of treaties held at Easton, he helped to clarify some of the matters dividing colonists and Indians. The final Easton Treaty of 1758 helped end most of the fighting in Pennsylvania when the Lenape made peace with the colony.

The Lenape also reconfirmed their subservience to the Iroquois, agreeing that the Six Nations could control their affairs. Pennsylvania promised to alter the terms of the Albany Congress purchase of 1754 by agreeing to keep white settlers out of the lands west of the Allegheny Mountains.

When news of this pact spread to western Pennsylvania, warfare rapidly declined throughout the province. Weiser could now return to a Tulpehocken Valley that no longer had to fear a sudden attack from out of the woods. And with the end of that threat came the end of Conrad Weiser's career as Pennsylvania's province interpreter. Easton in 1758 was his last treaty with the Indians.

Also in 1758, Weiser helped pacify Pennsylvania by organizing a wagon train of food and supplies for the Forbes Expedition on its westward advance. When this powerful British force approached the Forks of the Ohio, the hopeless French defenders blew up Fort Duquesne and abandoned the site.

THE DEATH OF CONRAD WEISER

After the struggles of the 1750s, which included the French and Indian War, his military duty, and the intensification of negotiations with participants who were less accommodating, Weiser came back to Tulpehocken to live in the manner he liked best: as a merchant, farmer, tanner, judge, husband, and father. Through a busy exchange of letters with Colonial officials, he was kept informed of developments in Indian affairs. Invited to travel to Fort Augusta, near today's Sunbury, Pennsylvania, in January 1760, he declined, saying that "I am at present lame and obliged to keep my Room." In May of that year, he was well enough to enjoy his son Sammy's wedding to Judith Levan, of Reading, and to drink some of the wine and punch purchased for the occasion.

There is little information regarding Weiser's final days. On July 12, 1760, he left Reading with Sir John Sinclair, a British official who was traveling toward Fort Pitt, the former French stronghold of Duquesne. Shortly after the journey started, Weiser suddenly became ill, suffering intense pain. At first "a little disordered," wrote Edward Shippen, an acquaintance, he was barely conscious when he was taken to the old Tulpehocken farmhouse. There "he continued ill & in a Stupid [lethargic] Condition till night & then expired." Based on the records of his earlier illnesses, it is likely that Weiser's death was caused by extreme complications from a kidney stone. Two days later, Conrad Weiser was buried in the family plot near the farmhouse, beside the graves of his father, several of his infant children, and a number of Indians who had died while visiting the Tulpehocken farm.

Changing circumstances in Colonial America, including the French and Indian War and Weiser's death, led to the end of the treaty system of negotiating relationships between Europeans and Native Americans. Although other

Conrad Weiser Rests in the center of a mall that was created in the 1920s and is now part of Conrad Weiser Homestead. A number of unmarked stones surrounding Weiser's grave are for Indians who had died in the area in Weiser's day.

interpreters were available, including Sammy Weiser, none of them seem to have had as much of an impact on the Indians as Conrad did. One of the clearest statements of Weiser's importance to the Indian-white relationship came from an old friend, the chief known as Seneca George. Speaking at a gathering in Easton in the summer of 1761, Seneca George lamented, "We . . . are at a great loss, and sit in darkness, as well as you, by the death of Conrad Weiser, as since his Death we cannot so well understand one another."

Conrad Weiser had a more intimate relationship with the Indians than almost any other of the two million Colonial Americans. He had walked their trails and eaten their food, spoken their language and slept in their longhouses. Some of his contemporaries feared that he was "soft on Indians," too sympathetic to the Indian point of view and too accepting of their culture.

Seneca George once described Weiser as "a great Man, and one-half a Seven Nation Indian [another group had joined the Iroquois League], & one-half an Englishman."

In the view of some modern scholars, Weiser would have been flattered by the second half of Seneca George's observation but dismayed by the first. Although comfortable in the woods of the frontier, he was more interested in making a home in the urban world that Reading promised to become. Weiser never wanted to become an Indian, finding little in their culture to admire. A devout Christian who had explored several varieties of organized belief, he saw no value in Indian religion. Firmly identifying with the dominant British culture, Weiser could see no lasting place for Indians in English Colonial society. In the end, he thought, the Indians would have to leave, and their land would be taken by Europeans.

History of Conrad Weiser Homestead

The Tulpehocken Creek flows in a southeasterly direction toward its merger with the Schuylkill River. In the Tulpehocken's lush valley, a German immigrant community started to develop in 1723 after a party of exiles from New York came south to establish homes and farms. Tulpehocken, the "Land of Turtles," was the property of the Lenape, who had been moved to this area by the Iroquois, their overlords. When Conrad Weiser and his wife and four children came to the area in 1729, the Lenape still held title to the valley, although Pennsylvania's governor, William Keith, had invited the Germans to settle the area. This was the origin of the Conrad Weiser Homestead.

AMONG THREE CULTURES

As German speakers, Conrad Weiser and his Tulpehocken neighbors were part of a distinct minority within William Penn's "Holy Experiment," a test of the premise that people of all faiths and all nationalities could live together peacefully and productively. Penn promised religious freedom to his settlers, refusing to establish an official faith for the colony. He also opened the province to immigrants from throughout Europe, reckoning that representatives of every nationality could contribute to its success. Although Pennsylvania eventually developed Colonial America's most diverse population, members of the province's major ethnic groups settled in distinct regions, or bands of settlement.

Penn's "Greene Country Towne," Philadelphia, was the hub of the region inhabited by the English and Welsh, who in the early years were predominantly Quaker. From their homes in the southeastern corner of the province, members of this group led Pennsylvania politically, economically, and socially. They were the first to arrive in the colony, and they were able to participate with the proprietor in establishing systems and structures that governed the rhythms of everyday life. Much of what this group created in Pennsylvania was based on British examples already very familiar to them.

A second large group of Colonial Pennsylvanians also came from the British Isles. These were the Scots-Irish, who began arriving in the province early

Weiser's Role in Pennsylvania Public Affairs was unique for a German immigrant in the eighteenth century. In the twentieth century, he became an icon of the Pennsylvania Dutch.

in the eighteenth century. Their ancestors had moved from Scotland to Ulster, in northern Ireland, during the reign of King James I in the early 1600s. A century later, these migrants sailed to America.

English speakers familiar with British customs, the Scots-Irish could participate with ease in the majority culture that dominated Pennsylvania. Some of them settled in pockets in the eastern counties, but many preferred to move westward, beyond the Susquehanna, to the very edge of settlement.

German-speaking people made up Colonial Pennsylvania's third major ethnic group. The first German immigrants arrived in the province only one year after William Penn's arrival, establishing the village of Germantown in the outskirts of Philadelphia in 1683. Some came to escape religious persecution; others hoped that life in Pennsylvania would offer prosperity and comfort not available to them in Europe. Most were from the southwestern portion of today's nation of Germany, which in the eighteenth century was a loose confederation of many kingdoms and states. German farmers, invited expressly by William Penn himself, came to the province from the lands surrounding the Rhine River, including the Palatinate, Württemberg, and Alsace. Some also came from the German-speaking cantons of Switzerland, where official regulations were making life difficult for religious dissenters.

Starting about 1720, Germans began streaming into Pennsylvania. Soon they constituted a major element in the colony's social mix, one that was unsettling to some English speakers, who feared losing their cultural identity to the hordes of newcomers from the European continent. Ben Franklin warned more than once about "Palatine boors"

Infant Mortality. Like many eighteenth-century farm families, the Weisers had several children. Also typical for the time was that more than half of the Weiser's offspring died before reaching adulthood.

and the "damn'd Dutch," fussing that Germans were dangerously close to overrunning the colony, but he also praised their work ethic and orderliness, and reckoned that they were making positive contributions to society.

Sandwiched between the English and Welsh communities to the east and the Scots-Irish on the west, the Germans filled in the middle sections of Colonial Pennsylvania. They were concentrated in parts of today's Northampton, Lehigh, Montgomery, Berks, Lebanon, and Lancaster Counties, sections where today, after the passage of three centuries, their cultural traditions are still very much alive. Many of those traditions are tied to the land, which they have farmed for three centuries and still yields bountiful crops.

THE WEISER FAMILY

During the forty years of their marriage, Conrad and Anna Eva Weiser had fourteen children, but only eight of them grew to adulthood. This was a typical ratio in Colonial times, when medical knowledge and care were minimal, and infant mortality rates were many times higher than today's. Anna Eva was fortunate to have survived, for many American women of her generation died during pregnancies and childbirths.

None of Weiser's children matched their father's prominence in public affairs or economic status. His oldest son, Philip, born in 1722 in New York, became a farmer, as did Frederick, born in 1728. Peter, the first Tulpehocken-born child (in 1730) made saddles and other leather goods. Only Sammy, born in 1735, shared his father's enthusiasm for Indian affairs. He lived with the Mohawks for a time, learned their language, and succeeded his father briefly as Pennsylvania's interpreter and Indian agent.

Weiser's oldest daughter, Anna Magdalena, died at age seventeen in 1742.

Henry Melchior Muhlenberg. Weiser's son-in-law was the father of Lutheranism in America. CONRAD WEISER HOMESTEAD

Her younger sister, Anna Maria, married a Lutheran minister named Henry Melchior Muhlenberg in 1745, when she was eighteen. Muhlenberg, a native of Einbeck in the German kingdom of Hanover, had a remarkable career as a developer of Lutheran congregations throughout the colonies. Weiser's third daughter, Margaret, died in 1777 at age forty-three. Her brother Benjamin, youngest of Weiser's surviving children, was still in his teens at the time of his father's death in 1760.

Among the eleven children born to Anna Maria and Henry Muhlenberg were three sons of note. These three grandsons of Conrad Weiser were all Lutheran clergymen. John Peter Gabriel, born in 1746, became a brigadier general of the Continental Army during the American Revolution. Frederick Augustus Conrad, four years younger, served in the Continental Congress during the Revolution and was the first speaker of the U.S. House of Representatives in 1789. A strong interest in science led the third grandson, Gotthilf Henry Ernest, born in 1753, to become a botanist.

THE WEISER FARM

Conrad Weiser's two hundred acres lay at the base of Eagle's Peak, a prominent feature that towered above the Tulpehocken Valley. After claiming his land, Weiser probably set up temporary housing for his family. Then, he faced the daunting task of turning a forest into a farm. Tree-covered Pennsylvania—after all, the name means "Penn's Woods"—had wonderfully fertile soil, but the farmer had to work to remove the undergrowth and the smaller trees. Colonial farmers killed a larger tree by girdling it—removing a wide strip of bark from around the trunk, and then waiting for the tree to die. Because

CONRAD WEISER'S INVENTORY

On July 30 and 31, 1760, less than three weeks after his death, three Berks County appraisers made a thorough list of Weiser's possessions at his home in Reading. While the inventory contains ordinary items, such as "an iron Stove," "two old Blanketts," "a Dung fork" and "Forty Eight Bushels of Oats," it also records many interesting objects that tell us more about Weiser's habits and values. He owned a "Cane Sword and pistols," "a fowling Piece," and "a Blunderbuss and twenty eight pounds of [gun]powder." For travel Weiser owned "a riding Horse and Saddle," "a Cart," and "a Sleigh and Geers," and he worked at "a Black Walnut Desk." A "large Map of Pennsylvania Framed" may have hung over the desk.

Weiser's "silver Watch" was worth 4 British pounds, and so was his "red Cow." "A Box with old Iron in it" was listed at 8 shillings, and "a Cask of Tallow," animal fat used to make soap or candles, was worth 4 shillings. He owned featherbeds, chaff (straw) beds, sheets, pillows, "Indian Blanketts," and "checked Coverlids" or coverlets. Weiser had eight "Table Cloaths" to place on his nine tables, and eighteen chairs to complement them. A prized possession must have been the "Chamber Organ & Musick Books belonging thereto."

Among the 150-odd books in Weiser's library were three German Bibles and one English. He owned law books, a dictionary, an atlas, and Voltaire's biography of King Charles XII of Sweden. Among his many religious books were six published by the Moravians and eight from the press at Ephrata, two hymnals, and a "German prayer book." To remind him of his European roots, Weiser kept the "Wirtemberg Geneology."

The greatest part of Weiser's estate lay in the form of loans he had made to neighbors and family members over the years. These unpaid debts, valued at more than 1,500 British pounds, were owed by fifty people and ranged in size from George Gabriel's 1-pound note to the 202-pound bond from Martin Kast and David Zeller. The total value of Weiser's property, excluding the real estate, was 2,641 pounds, 17 shillings, a huge sum for that era.

A Spoon Once Owned by Conrad Weiser.

removing the stumps took an enormous amount of time and energy, farmers usually let them stay in the fields, plowing and planting around them until they eventually rotted away.

Because corn—a gift from the Indians—was easy to grow and gave abundant yields, it was eighteenth-century America's most important crop. Weiser grew it, and he also reaped harvests of wheat, oats, barley, grapes, and rye. He grew hay for his horses and cattle, and flax to turn into linen and linseed oil. His hemp was made into rope or bagging. In his orchard, Weiser tended peach, apple, and cherry trees. The sheep yielded wool and mutton, and pork came from the hogs that roamed the farm.

Typical Pennsylvania German farmers followed a crop-rotation system that called for varying the crops planted in each field according to a fixed schedule. This technique replenished the soil by replacing nutrients consumed during the growing season. One year in the cycle called for growing clover, which was then plowed under; during another summer, a field could lie idle, or fallow. The

Germans spread earth-enhancing animal manure and lime on their fields, too.

Over the years, Weiser's landholdings in Tulpehocken grew to encompass nearly nine hundred acres. On a remote section of the farm, he established a tannery for turning hides and skins from cattle, sheep, and deer into leather. An extremely important product in the years before synthetics, plastics, and rubber, leather was made into footwear, belts, hats, trousers, jackets, saddles, and harnesses. In the 1750s, Weiser's son Peter, his first Pennsylvania-born child, worked as a saddle maker in Reading.

At the tannery, the skins were cleaned with lye before being put into a box that was dug into the earth. Covered with layers of crushed oak or hemlock bark, the skins were then soaked with water and allowed to steep in their chemical bath for six months to two years. When the tanner removed the skins, he washed them and hung them to dry. Repeated rubbing and rolling finished the job, making the leather pliable. A glance at Weiser's account book reveals the busy pace of activity at the tannery and indicates its place in his financial affairs. A steady customer was Peter,

Weiser's son, who took three "sides" of leather in December 1754. One was "on account of the saddle," and the other two were "on account of skinning beefs of which he still has credit."

Weiser also stocked provisions, selling rum, nails, molasses, and tobacco to his neighbors. He bought and sold animals, soap, meat, and other products. Because of his prominence in business, local politics, and Indian affairs, his Tulpehocken farm became a noted landmark. The home and its environs became known as "Weiser's," and that name appears on some early maps of the region. It became a gathering place for a fascinating array of characters: Indians encamped in a meadow, traders swapping goods and money, scientists preparing for trips into the woods, missionaries about to head north in search of converts.

PUBLIC AFFAIRS

Weiser's participation in public life was not restricted to his work as a negotiator with the Indians. Possibly because he had seen his father take leadership posts in the Schoharie settlement, Weiser was prompted to become involved in public

The Tulpehocken. The fertile land of the valley is still heavily farmed in the present. In the distance is Eagle's Peak, which Weiser crossed on his journeys north.

Weiser House, Reading.
CONRAD WEISER HOMESTEAD

matters in the Tulpehocken community. One of his first duties was serving as an overseer of the poor in his township. He also held the post of ranger, which required him to round up stray animals and hold them until their owners appeared to claim them. In March 1743, Weiser posted a notice in the *Pennsylvania Gazette* that he was holding fifteen runaway horses; apparently some early Pennsylvanians were a bit lax about animal security.

When Weiser was appointed to the post of justice of the peace in 1741, he entered the world of law and order at a basic, but highly significant, level. As a justice, he was a minor judge who could conduct civil and criminal trials, supervise local sheriffs, and issue various licenses. He dealt with problems involving indentured servants. And because slavery was legal in Pennsylvania—a gradual abolition law was passed in 1780—he also had to handle the cases of runaway slaves. Weiser received income by charging fees for his services; he also performed marriages.

To participate in civic affairs at any level beyond the most local, Pennsylvania's German-born settlers had to master English, become naturalized citizens, and swear an oath of allegiance to the British king. For many newcomers, these steps were difficult to take. But because Weiser welcomed the chance to become a leader in his adopted homeland, he was naturalized in 1744.

Few Germans were active in Pennsylvania politics in Weiser's day. Those who voted usually supported the Quaker faction that dominated the provincial legislature. Through his contacts with Colonial leaders, Weiser became involved with the rival Proprietary party, made up of the Penn family and its supporters. (Although William Penn was a prominent Quaker, his sons were Anglicans.) A key policy difference between the two groups was the defense issue, with the pacifist Quakers opposing the military preparedness that the Proprietaries called for.

Weiser jumped into political campaigning in 1741, when he wrote a pamphlet asking his fellow Germans to support the Penns in an upcoming election. *A Serious and Sensible Advice to Our Countrymen ye Germans in America* had a weighty title, but it did not swing many German votes to the Proprietary side. Weiser unsuccessfully ran for a seat in the Pennsylvania legislature in 1741, 1747, and 1756.

READING, PENNSYLVANIA

Weiser had arrived in Pennsylvania just as the colony was ending a period of slow growth and entering a dynamic phase of rapid increase. A characteristic of this era was the founding of a series of new towns situated at key points in the countryside. Although none would compete with the political and economic might of Philadelphia, which was rapidly becoming Colonial America's largest city, these new communities supported craftsmen and merchants, became exchange points for farm crops, had schools and churches, published newspapers, and stimulated further growth in their regions. Lancaster was founded in 1730, York in 1741, and both Easton and Carlisle in 1752.

In 1748, Proprietor Thomas Penn picked a site about thirteen miles east of Weiser's farm, where the Tulpehocken Creek flows into the Schuylkill River, for the town of Reading. Only fifty-five miles from Philadelphia, Reading was a two-day wagon ride from the capital. Weiser joined a small group of men who were given the assignment of transforming Penn's dreams of creating this new town into reality.

The planners had Reading carefully surveyed and divided into lots, putting in place a rectangular gridwork of streets similar to the one William Penn had created for Philadelphia. Weiser bought two lots on Penn Square, at the town's center,

and several more at other locations. In 1751, his Penn Square house became Reading's first home. He lived there part-time, using the house as the base for his activities as a provisioning agent.

Weiser was the driving force behind the creation of Berks County. He filed petitions, hired mapmakers, and traveled to Philadelphia many times in this effort. According to his journal, he spent 40 pounds of his own funds by the time the county was established in 1752. He also obtained the post of president judge when the new county's court system was initiated.

WEISER'S SPIRITUAL PATH
Conrad Weiser, the man of business affairs, diplomacy, and community service, also had a strong spiritual side. He began in the Lutheran creed of his family in Württemberg, continuing this asso-

Ephrata Cloister. Weiser lived and worshiped at Ephrata for a brief time in the early 1740s. He departed three years before Bethania, *a dormitory for the celibate brothers, was built. The building deteriorated through the years and had to be torn down. The surviving buildings at Ephrata Cloister are open to the public as part of a state historic site administered by the Pennsylvania Historical and Museum Commission.* PENNSYLVANIA STATE ARCHIVES (RG-13)

ciation in the New World. After arriving in the Tulpehocken settlement in 1729, he took an active part in the life of the Lutheran parish in the community. At this time, he also became friendly with Peter Miller, a young pastor who led a German Reformed congregation in Tulpehocken. These two denominations, Lutheran and Reformed (the "Church People"), accounted for nine-tenths of the Pennsylvania Germans who participated in religious activities. The remaining tenth, called the "Sect People," were divided among a variety of faiths including German Baptist, Mennonite, Amish, Moravian, and Schwenkfelder.

In the early 1730s, the Tulpehocken region experienced a period of intense religious enthusiasm and questioning known as "the Confusion." At this time people examined their faiths, measured them against competing creeds, and looked for new avenues to spiritual growth. During this period, Weiser met a charismatic preacher named Conrad Beissel, who was then forming a religious community at Ephrata, twenty miles south of Tulpehocken in the Cocalico Valley. Beissel's message was so strong, and his personality so compelling, that both Weiser and his friend Miller, as well as others in the Tulpehocken, converted to his teaching.

Beissel, an immigrant from the German Palatinate who was five years older than Weiser, presented a unique faith system that promised personal union with God. To achieve this divine connection, he proclaimed, a believer had to become totally absorbed in a life of contemplation, preparation, and discipline. In Beissel's theology, marriage was a distraction from this pursuit. It was better, he said, to remain celibate, forsaking all sexual activity.

Beissel also held that material comforts were unnecessary because they interfered with spiritual growth. This belief led some of his followers to restrict their diets to a few simple foods eaten only once a day, sleep on narrow wooden benches, and shun luxuries of any kind. The most devoted of Beissel's followers joined him at Ephrata, where a community that was following his system was developing. At its height, which occurred around 1750, Ephrata was a community of about three hundred people, including celibates who lived in Beissel's settlement and the more numerous householders, who worshiped there but lived on their own farms. Because Beissel and many of his followers had once been connected with the German Baptist church, and because they now observed the Saturday Sabbath, they became known as German Seventh-Day Baptists.

Some of Weiser's family moved to Ephrata with him, and although Anna Eva soon left to return to the Tulpehocken home, Conrad remained a member of the community for several years; however, he probably lived at Ephrata for less than two years. His daughter Anna Magdalena died at Ephrata in 1742 when she was only seventeen. Just at the time he was becoming involved with Pennsylvania's Indian policy, Weiser took an active part in the affairs of his new home. He went on several evangelizing trips to German-American communities in the middle colonies in search of new members. On other trips, Weiser went alone, over the mountain to Tulpehocken and home, where he could maintain his marital ties.

It was not long before Weiser was drawn away from Ephrata's contemplative life back into the world of business, politics, and diplomacy. He also disagreed with Beissel's inflexible leadership style, which similarly rankled other members of the community from time to time. (By contrast, Peter Miller found contentment at Ephrata, living there for the rest of his life.) In his 1743 letter of resignation, Weiser stated his intentions bluntly: "I take leave of your young, but already decrepit sect, and I desire henceforth to be treated as a stranger."

Weiser was also involved for a time with the Moravians, another German sect, which traced its ancestry to fifteenth-century reformers in what is now primarily the Czech Republic. By Weiser's time, the Moravians had become an evangelical group who wanted to minimize the differences among the German faiths and unite all of the Pennsylvania Germans into one spiritual community. He became familiar with many Moravian leaders, including Count Nicholas Ludwig von Zinzendorf, the head of the church. Moravian missionaries also traveled with Weiser over Pennsylvania's formidable mountain ranges, and in 1745, two of them, August Gottlieb Spangenberg and

David Zeisberger, trekked with him all the way to Onondaga in the center of the Iroquois homeland.

Weiser's spiritual journey led him back to his Lutheran roots by the late 1740s. As one of the planners of the new town of Reading, he was also a founder of that community's Trinity Lutheran Church in 1751. He composed a hymn that was sung at the church's dedication. At Weiser's funeral in July 1760, his Lutheran pastor in Tulpehocken preached the sermon.

THE HOMESTEAD IN LATER YEARS AND THE MOVEMENT TO HONOR WEISER

In Weiser's 1760 will, the 890-acre farm in Tulpehocken was divided among four of his sons. Frederick, the second oldest, worked the land, including the section where the homestead is situated, for some time, followed by his son, another Conrad. In the ensuing years, the Weiser children moved away, some to other land their father had owned north and west of Tulpehocken, near Selinsgrove. After a nonrelative, John Scheetz, pur-

The Farmhouse, right, *which now serves as the visitor center for Conrad Weiser Homestead, was built by John Scheetz, who purchased the land in 1834.* LESTER P. BREININGER JR. COLLECTION

chased the farm in the nineteenth century, he built a large stone farmhouse beside the old Weiser home, which he probably used as a summer kitchen.

As America entered the industrial age, following the Civil War, the Pennsylvania German community began to lose some of its uniqueness. No longer primarily a simple farming folk, the Pennsylvania Germans were now active in business, politics, and many other aspects of American life. Some of them began to look back to the past to affirm the differences that had separated their ancestors from the mainstream English culture of Colonial days. They proudly emphasized the positive aspects and numerous contributions of the early German community. The Pennsylvania German Society was established in 1891 to record and preserve the history of the ethnic group.

In 1876, Rev. C. Z. Weiser, a descendant of Conrad's, published a biography of Conrad Weiser that was widely read in Berks County and across Pennsylvania. Later the book was reprinted in a special edition designed for use in the public schools. Berks County educators also initiated, in 1893, an activity known as Conrad Weiser Day to honor the memory of the man who was then seen as the county's foremost founding citizen. The highlight of a 1907 teachers' meeting in Reading was the placing of a bronze plaque at the site of Weiser's old house on Penn Square. In 1909, a large stone monument honoring Conrad Weiser was installed in the borough of

Conrad Weiser Day was a Berks County celebration begun in 1893 to commemorate the county's founder.

Womelsdorf, the town that lies just west of the old homestead.

World War I embroiled America in its first major overseas conflict, and soon the Roaring Twenties brought changes that transformed the country. Almost overnight, it seemed, homes got electricity, household appliances proliferated, and telephone service became commonplace. America took to the road, as automobiles, initially playthings for the wealthy, now became affordable for the average family. The spirit of the age was one of buoyant optimism. America was becoming modern.

Some Americans felt, however, that becoming modern did not mean forgetting the past. Since the public mind equated history with remembering anniversaries of events and honoring the exploits of exceptional people, this was also a decade in which new memorials were created to past heroes. For Berks County, that hero was Conrad Weiser.

Remembering that their ancestors had created the Tulpehocken settlement in 1723, residents of the valley held a bicentennial commemoration in 1923. Out of this celebration came a desire to do something to honor Tulpehocken's most prominent early citizen, Conrad Weiser, whose home, or what was left of it, still stood on its original spot. The community decided to refurbish the house and create a scenic park around it.

Conrad Weiser Monument was originally erected in Womelsdorf in 1909 but was later moved to the park. LESTER P. BREININGER JR. COLLECTION

The Conrad Weiser Memorial Park Association was formed by local businesspeople, professionals, and educators to take charge of the project. The association successfully negotiated with the current landowner, LeRoy Valentine, coincidentally a Weiser descendant, for the house and twenty acres. Berks County agreed to supplement the funds raised by the association to pay for the house's restoration. To plan the surrounding memorial park, the association hired America's best-known landscape architecture firm, Olmsted Brothers of Brookline, Massachusetts.

John Charles Olmsted and Frederick Law Olmsted Jr. were the sons of Frederick Law Olmsted, America's first prominent landscape architect. The senior Olmsted designed New York's Central Park and the grounds of George Washington Vanderbilt's immense Biltmore House near Asheville, North Carolina. He also planned urban parks in Boston, Louisville, Atlanta, and Buffalo as well as college campuses, hospital grounds, zoos, suburbs, and private estates. Because of his love of nature and strong feelings about preserving open spaces, Olmsted was one of the early promoters of our national park system. After his retirement in 1895, his sons took over the firm.

Frederick Jr. was the head of Olmsted Brothers in the 1920s. He shared his father's enthusiasm for the beauty of wilderness, and he also recognized the need for careful planning for orderly growth in both urban and rural areas. Among his greatest accomplishments were designs for Acadia, Everglades, and Yosemite National Parks, and his creation of the National Mall, the great expanse between the Capitol and the Lincoln Memorial in Washington, DC.

In a series of letters to the architects written in 1925 and 1926, the directors of the association gave clear directions

*A **Tornado** ravaged the Weiser House in 1904.* LESTER P. BREININGER JR. COLLECTION

about their vision for the treatment of Conrad Weiser's Memorial Park. They wanted "a simple, dignified, historical setting forth of this old Colonial homestead" that would "preserve the simplicity and rusticity of the buildings and surroundings as near as these were in Weiser's day." Despite the reference to a historical setting, the association did not want to re-create a working Colonial-era farm complete with wheat fields, meadows, orchard, outbuildings, animal pens, and a tannery. Instead, the group hoped to turn the site into a scenic park by sculpting the landscape into a thing of beauty.

The design submitted by a member of Olmsted Brothers' large staff met this objective. It placed the old Weiser home, its springhouse, and an adjacent nineteenth-century farmhouse in the midst of a carefully manufactured environment that featured long, winding driveways, a charming artificial lake, and many groves of trees and other plantings. The Weiser burial plot, which stood on a small rise just east of the historic buildings, was prominently incorporated into the design. Wide expanses of grassy lawn provided areas for picnicking, play, or rest.

The 1909 stone monument was moved from Womelsdorf and given a prominent spot in a tree-lined "mall" that was a focal point of the park. A memorial boulder to Shikellamy, Weiser's Iroquois colleague, traveling companion, and shaper of Pennsylvania's Indian policy, was also placed in this formal section of the park (a lifelike statue of Shikellamy was put on the boulder in the 1930s). Throughout the site, many smaller memorials honored other noted Pennsylvanians, especially people from the Tulpehocken and Berks County regions, or acknowledged those who had contributed to the creation of the park.

Conrad Weiser's farmhouse, then almost two centuries old, had suffered from neglect, a tornado, and a fire. Little remained of its original interior, although the solid limestone shell of its thick, sturdy walls was mostly intact. The commissioners of Berks County agreed to use public funds to restore the house so that the Memorial Association could devote all of its resources to the creation of the rest of the park.

Because the concept of restoring old buildings was a new idea in the 1920s, there were few guidelines to follow or techniques to use. Many existing structures that dated from the period of the Weiser house had been modified, enhanced, or adapted over the years, and scholars had not yet begun careful studies that could indicate what Colonial homes might have looked like when they were brand new. The restorers had little documentation, other than the house itself, to work with—no blueprints or sketches, no photographs, and practically no written descriptions of any significance.

The source that most profoundly guided the house's restoration was a style of architecture, popular in America since the early 1900s, known as Colonial Revival. This type of house design was inspired by the Georgian and Federal styles popular in America in the decades preceding and following the American Revolution. The Colonial Revival style broke completely from the nineteenth-century pattern of fanciful Victorian houses with towers, turrets, ornate gingerbread woodwork, and asymmetrical facades. Instead, homes had a retro look that imitated the design features of James River plantation residences, stately Philadelphia row houses, or classical homes of New England fishing villages.

Today the Conrad Weiser house is seen as a prime example of a Colonial Revival restoration of a Colonial home—a 1920s interpretation of what a 1720s Pennsylvania German dwelling would have looked like. It documents an important early step in both recognizing the importance of preserving a landmark in Pennsylvania's history and carrying out this restoration based on assumptions and attitudes of the 1920s.

When Conrad Weiser Memorial Park was dedicated on September 1, 1928, a crowd of twenty-five thousand gathered to watch the proceedings. Its mission accomplished, the association then went out of existence, transferring ownership of the site to the Commonwealth of Pennsylvania. Today the Conrad Weiser Homestead is administered by the Pennsylvania Historical and Museum Commission, which interprets Conrad Weiser's legacy to the modern world.

The Dedication of Conrad Weiser Memorial Park was held on September 1, 1928.

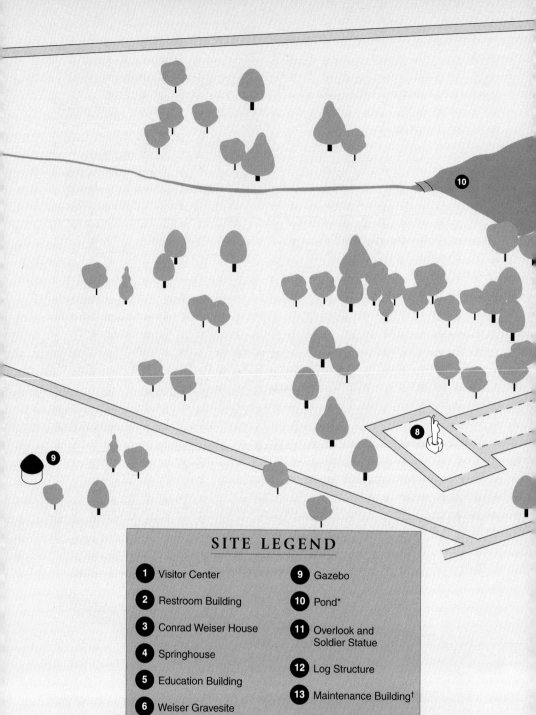

SITE LEGEND

1	Visitor Center	**9**	Gazebo
2	Restroom Building	**10**	Pond*
3	Conrad Weiser House	**11**	Overlook and Soldier Statue
4	Springhouse	**12**	Log Structure
5	Education Building	**13**	Maintenance Building†
6	Weiser Gravesite	🚻	Restrooms
7	Conrad Weiser Monument		* No swimming or fishing allowed
8	Shikellamy Statue		† Not open to the public

Visiting the Site

1 VISITOR CENTER

This solid Pennsylvania German limestone farmhouse was built by John Scheetz, who bought the Weiser farm in 1834. The Scheetz family lived in this large dwelling and probably used the old Weiser House as a separate summer kitchen, a common practice of rural households in this part of Pennsylvania. Scheetz also built the great stone barn that stands across the road from the parking area; it is now privately owned as part of a commercial enterprise and is not part of the historic site.

In this building, visitors may purchase admission tickets and browse the orientation exhibit that establishes Conrad Weiser's place in the early history of Pennsylvania. The Museum Shop presents a wide range of books and pamphlets relating to American Indian cultures, Colonial Pennsylvania, Pennsylvania German society, and military activities of the eighteenth century.

2 RESTROOM BUILDING

The stone building (not pictured), which houses public lavatories, was part of the 1920s Olmsted plan. Like other structures added to the grounds in the twentieth century, it was constructed of native Pennsylvania limestone and was designed to harmonize with the appearance and scale of the old Weiser home.

3 CONRAD WEISER HOUSE

Not long after they moved to the Tulpehocken Valley from the colony of New York, Conrad and Anna Eva Weiser built a stone farmhouse on land where the soil was rich. Overhead towered eleven-hundred-foot Eagle's Peak, a sweet spring bubbled nearby, and a new road that would lead to the city of Philadelphia was close at hand. Paul Wallace, Weiser's most exacting biographer, describes the house succinctly: "square, solid, simple in plan."

The house you see today was restored in the 1920s in the Colonial Revival style. As you stand facing the house, note that it actually contains two sections. The Weisers built the older part, the "square"

left-hand portion, which includes the front door, to replace the crude log cabin that was their temporary home. Its thick limestone walls enclosed one main room, which functioned as a combination kitchen, dining area, and sitting room. Although eighteenth-century Pennsylvania German homes typically had three or four rooms, the one-room plan, which this house features, was common in the earliest settlements.

The large gable fireplace, complete with bake oven, supplied heat for cooking and warmed the house in cold weather. Food could be stored in the cool cellar below. Overhead, beneath the eaves, were sleeping quarters for the

children, servants, or visitors. The attic was used for dry food storage.

The second section, the room closer to the Scheetz House, may have been added by Weiser but was most likely built by a nineteenth-century owner. It completes the symmetry of the home, balancing the proportions of the earlier structure, while changing the square shape into a rectangle. Care was taken to match the exterior stonework and roof line of the older portion when this section was added. It created additional living space, quite possibly for an office, as seen in the current interpretation.

The Weiser House is furnished with eighteenth-century Pennsylvania German pieces that illustrate the wide range of tasks and interests of farm families years ago. Although the furnishings are not original to the site, all are of the age and type that would have been found here in the Weisers' day. Baking bread, preserving food by pickling or salting, and turning flax into linen cloth were only a few of the common activities in those days. Other objects, such as the large German Bible, suggest Weiser's profound interest in religion. The desk, with its quill pens and ledgers, represents the hours he spent in writing summaries of his meetings with the Indians, keeping business accounts, and rendering decisions in the minor court cases he heard as a justice of the peace.

The Weiser farm lay at the southern end of the Tulpehocken pathway that led through forests, over mountains, and across rivers to the Indian village of Shamokin. Thus it was from this house that Conrad began his treks northward to see Shikellamy, the Iroquois spokesman. Missionaries, statesmen, scientists, and other adventurers who accompanied Weiser on his journeys knew the home well. So did Indians from Onondaga, in the center of New York's Iroquois homeland, who camped here while on their way to Philadelphia, Annapolis, or Williamsburg.

④ SPRINGHOUSE

Large Colonial-era farms like Weiser's had many smaller structures, such as privies, storage sheds, barns, pens for animals, blacksmith shops, and smokehouses. The Weiser farm also contained a building or buildings that housed the tannery. This springhouse is the only surviving support building that remains from the site's era of farming.

Made primarily of native stone, the building stands on top of a spring whose cold, clear water was used to chill perishable food items, as the Colonial era had no mechanical refrigeration. Also the surest source of pure drinking water on the farm, the spring played a vital role in the family's survival. Because the building has an oven on its gable wall, it is likely that it was also used as a bakehouse. The family probably stored grain or other items in large barrels on the upper floor.

5 EDUCATION BUILDING

Originally built in the 1930s, this building (not pictured) houses exhibits and is used for public and school programs.

6 WEISER GRAVESITE

This burial plot holds the remains of Conrad Weiser and of his father, Johan Conrad, who died here in 1746. It is not certain whether Anna Eva also rests here. Some of the Weiser children who died in infancy are also probably interred here. In addition, there are clues that a number of Iroquois who died while visiting the Weisers are also buried at this site.

Conrad's gravestone, the only legible one presently on view, is written in the German of his native Württemberg. The epitaph calls him "the late highly esteemed magistrate" and tells us he died on July 13, 1760, at the age of sixty-four.

Small family graveyards like this one are common along the backroads of the Pennsylvania German farm country. They serve as visible reminders of the generations who have been linked to the land and to one another through the land.

7 THE CONRAD WEISER MONUMENT

In the late nineteenth and early twentieth centuries, citizens of Berks County began to search for ways to honor Conrad Weiser. A prominent fraternal society, the Patriotic Order Sons of America, which had fifty-four clubs in the county, commissioned this stone monument and installed it in the nearby borough of Womelsdorf in 1909. After the creation of Conrad Weiser Memorial Park, the obelisk was brought to its present location. The sculptor represented the Iroquois, Lenape, and other Indians of Pennsylvania with a tepee more correctly associated with Indians of the Great Plains. A rectangular wooden longhouse structure like the one Weiser slept in throughout the cold winter of 1713 would have been more historically accurate.

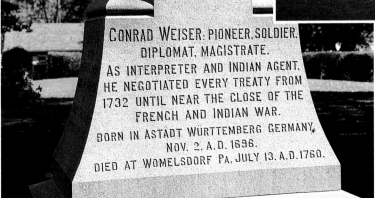

CONRAD WEISER: PIONEER, SOLDIER, DIPLOMAT, MAGISTRATE. AS INTERPRETER AND INDIAN AGENT, HE NEGOTIATED EVERY TREATY FROM 1732 UNTIL NEAR THE CLOSE OF THE FRENCH AND INDIAN WAR. BORN IN ASTADT WÜRTTEMBERG GERMANY, NOV. 2. A.D. 1696. DIED AT WOMELSDORF PA, JULY 13. A.D. 1760.

8 SHIKELLAMY STATUE

Shikellamy was the Iroquois diplomat who worked with Weiser to maintain peace between the colony of Pennsylvania and its Indian neighbors. An Oneida leader known as "Our Enlightener," Shikellamy was sent by the Iroquois to oversee the tribes they had conquered in Pennsylvania. He made many trips up and down the Tulpehocken Path, which ran over the "Endless Hills" from his home of Shamokin (now Sunbury) to Weiser's farm. The two collaborated from 1731 to 1748 and were instrumental in establishing Pennsylvania's "new Indian policy" of dealing only with the Iroquois in matters concerning the colony's Indian relationships.

New York sculptor Joseph Pollia created the statue in 1930. The upraised arm and hand are a traditional Iroquois gesture of friendship, representing Shikellamy's personal connection with Weiser. The boulder with its bronze figure was placed in the Olmsted plan's square "exterior room," which was linked to the Weiser grave circle by a long, tree-lined mall. This use of open spaces marked off by linear plantings is frequently found in Olmsted designs. It represents a significant departure from a truly natural landscape.

9 GAZEBO

From its high spot near the western edge of the Homestead, the gazebo provides clear views of the landscape with its winding, serpentine drives, meandering paths, groves of stately trees, and open fields. These are all elements typical of Olmsted parks as found in cities and towns across America.

10 POND

This man-made pond can be enjoyed from the handsome stone bridge that abuts it. It is fed by natural springs and was designed by the landscape architects to beautify the park.

11 OVERLOOK AND SOLDIER STATUE

To honor local men, "Heroes of the Tulpehocken," who served in World War I (1914–18), this statue of an American infantry soldier, or "doughboy," was installed here in 1926. It was erected by the Memorial Park Association, which established this site to pay tribute not only to the region's most prominent citizen of the Colonial era, but also to the many men from the community who were involved in America's first transoceanic war of the twentieth century.

12 LOG STRUCTURE

This small cabin was brought to this site in 1927 by the Memorial Park Association. Its age, original location, and use have not been determined.

For information on hours, tours, programs, and activities at Conrad Weiser Homestead, visit **www.phmc.state.pa.us** or call **610-589-2934**.

Further Reading

Albright, Raymond W. *Two Centuries of Reading, Pa.: 1748–1948*. Reading, Pa.: Historical Society of Berks County, 1948.

Fogelman, Aaron Spencer. *Hopeful Journeys: German Immigration, Settlement, and Political Culture in Colonial America, 1717–1775*. Philadelphia: University of Pennsylvania Press, 1996.

Graymont, Barbara. *The Iroquois*. New York: Chelsea House, 1998.

Griffing, Robert. *The Art of Robert Griffing: His Journey into the Eastern Frontier*. Ashville, N.Y.: East/West Visions, 2000.

Grumet, Robert S., ed. *Northeastern Indian Lives, 1632–1816*. Amherst: University of Massachusetts Press, 1996.

Jacobs, Wilbur R. *Dispossessing the American Indian: Indians and Whites on the Colonial Frontier*. Norman: University of Oklahoma Press, 1985.

Kelly, Joseph J., Jr. *Pennsylvania: The Colonial Years, 1681–1776*. Garden City, N.Y.: Doubleday and Company, 1980.

Merrell, James H. *Into the American Woods: Negotiators on the Pennsylvania Frontier*. New York: W. W. Norton and Company, 1999.

Neff, Larry M., and Frederick S. Weiser, eds. *The Account Book of Conrad Weiser, Berks County, Pennsylvania, 1746–1760*. Breinigsville, Pa.: Pennsylvania German Society, 1981.

Pendleton, Philip E. "Finding a Light in the Forest: Conrad Weiser Homestead," *Pennsylvania Heritage* (Summer 1996), 12–19.

Richter, Daniel K. *The Ordeal of the Longhouse: The Peoples of the Iroquois League in the Era of European Colonization*. Chapel Hill: University of North Carolina Press, 1992.

Wallace, Paul A. W. *Conrad Weiser: Friend of Colonist and Mohawk*. New York: Russell and Russell, 1945.

———. *Indians in Pennsylvania*. 2nd ed. Harrisburg: Pennsylvania Historical and Museum Commission, 1981.

———. *Indian Paths of Pennsylvania*. Harrisburg: Pennsylvania Historical and Museum Commission, 1993.

Weiser, Frederick S., ed. *Weiser Families in America*. 2 vols. New Oxford, Pa.: Johann Conrad Weiser Family Association, 1997.